**SELF-LOVE JOURNAL**
ISBN Hardcover: 979-8-3482-2997-9
ISBN Paperback: 979-8-3482-3004-3

**SELF-LOVE JOURNAL with 7-SHIFT PLANNER**
ISBN Hardcover: 979-8-3482-3012-8
ISBN Paperback: 979-8-3482-3023-4

# My Self-Love Notes
### The Most Important Relationship Is the One You Have with Yourself
### Self-Love Is a Daily Practice

# My Self-Love Notes
### The Most Important Relationship Is the One You Have with Yourself
### Self-Love Is a Daily Practice

"You Don't Find Love, You Create Love" Sharon Esther Lampert

# My Self-Love Notes
### The Most Important Relationship Is the One You Have with Yourself
### Self-Love Is a Daily Practice

"You Don't Find Love, You Create Love" Sharon Esther Lampert

# My Self-Love Notes
### The Most Important Relationship Is the One You Have with Yourself
### Self-Love Is a Daily Practice

"You Can't Find Love, You Create Love" Sharon Esther Lampert

# My Self-Love Notes
### The Most Important Relationship Is the One You Have with Yourself
### Self-Love Is a Daily Practice

# My Self-Love Notes
## The Most Important Relationship Is the One You Have with Yourself
## Self-Love Is a Daily Practice

# My Self-Love Notes
## The Most Important Relationship Is the One You Have with Yourself
## Self-Love Is a Daily Practice

"You Don't Find Love – You Create Love" Sharon Esther Lampert

# My Self-Love Notes
## The Most Important Relationship Is the One You Have with Yourself
## Self-Love Is a Daily Practice

"You Don't Find Love, You Create Love" Sharon Esther Lampert

# My Self-Love Notes
## The Most Important Relationship Is the One You Have with Yourself
## Self-Love Is a Daily Practice

# My Self-Love Notes
### The Most Important Relationship Is the One You Have with Yourself
### Self-Love Is a Daily Practice

"You Don't Find Love, You Create Love" Sharon Esther Lampert

# My Self-Love Notes
## The Most Important Relationship Is the One You Have with Yourself
## Self-Love Is a Daily Practice

"You Don't Find Love, You Create Love" Sharon Esther Lampert

# My Self-Love Notes
## The Most Important Relationship Is the One You Have with Yourself
## Self-Love Is a Daily Practice

# My Self-Love Notes
## The Most Important Relationship Is the One You Have with Yourself
## Self-Love Is a Daily Practice

"You Don't Find Love, You Create Love" Sharon Esther Lampert

# My Self-Love Notes
### The Most Important Relationship Is the One You Have with Yourself
### Self-Love Is a Daily Practice

"You Don't Find Love, You Create Love" Sharon Esther Lampert

# My Self-Love Notes
## The Most Important Relationship Is the One You Have with Yourself
## Self-Love Is a Daily Practice

# My Self-Love Notes
## The Most Important Relationship Is the One You Have with Yourself
## Self-Love Is a Daily Practice

"You Don't Find Love, You Create Love" Sharon Esther Lampert

# My Self-Love Notes
## The Most Important Relationship Is the One You Have with Yourself
## Self-Love Is a Daily Practice

"You Don't Find Love, You Create Love" Sharon Esther Lampert

# My Self-Love Notes
## The Most Important Relationship Is the One You Have with Yourself
## Self-Love Is a Daily Practice

"You Don't Find Love, You Create Love" Sharon Esther Lampert

# My Self-Love Notes
## The Most Important Relationship Is the One You Have with Yourself
## Self-Love Is a Daily Practice

"You Don't Find Love, You Create Love." Sharon Esther Lampert

# My Self-Love Notes
## The Most Important Relationship Is the One You Have with Yourself
## Self-Love Is a Daily Practice

"You Don't Find Love, You Create Love" Sharon Esther Lampert

# My Self-Love Notes
### The Most Important Relationship Is the One You Have with Yourself
### Self-Love Is a Daily Practice

"You Don't Find Love, You Create Love" Sharon Esther Lampert

# My Self-Love Notes
### The Most Important Relationship Is the One You Have with Yourself
### Self-Love Is a Daily Practice

"You Don't Find Love, You Create Love" Sharon Esther Lampert

# My Self-Love Notes
## The Most Important Relationship Is the One You Have with Yourself
## Self-Love Is a Daily Practice

"You Don't Find Love, You Create Love" Sharon Esther Lampert

# My Self-Love Notes
## The Most Important Relationship Is the One You Have with Yourself
## Self-Love Is a Daily Practice

"You Don't Find Love, You Create Love" Sharon Esther Lampert

# My Self-Love Notes
### The Most Important Relationship Is the One You Have with Yourself
### Self-Love Is a Daily Practice

"You Don't Find Love, You Create Love" Sharon Esther Lampert

# My Self-Love Notes
## The Most Important Relationship Is the One You Have with Yourself
## Self-Love Is a Daily Practice

"You Don't Find Love, You Create Love" Sharon Esther Lampert

# My Self-Love Notes
## The Most Important Relationship Is the One You Have with Yourself
## Self-Love Is a Daily Practice

"You Don't Find Love, You Create Love" Sharon Esther Lampert

# My Self-Love Notes
## The Most Important Relationship Is the One You Have with Yourself
## Self-Love Is a Daily Practice

"You Don't Find Love, You Create Love" Sharon Esther Lampert

# My Self-Love Notes
## The Most Important Relationship Is the One You Have with Yourself
## Self-Love Is a Daily Practice

"You Don't Find Love, You Create Love" Sharon Esther Lampert

# My Self-Love Notes
### The Most Important Relationship Is the One You Have with Yourself
### Self-Love Is a Daily Practice

"You Don't Find Love, You Create Love" Sharon Esther Lampert

# My Self-Love Notes
## The Most Important Relationship Is the One You Have with Yourself
## Self-Love Is a Daily Practice

"You Don't Find Love, You Create Love" Sharon Esther Lampert

# My Self-Love Notes
### The Most Important Relationship Is the One You Have with Yourself
### Self-Love Is a Daily Practice

"You Don't Find Love, You Create Love" Sharon Esther Lampert

# My Self-Love Notes
## The Most Important Relationship Is the One You Have with Yourself
## Self-Love Is a Daily Practice

"You Don't Find Love, You Create Love" Sharon Esther Lampert

# My Self-Love Notes
## The Most Important Relationship Is the One You Have with Yourself
## Self-Love Is a Daily Practice

"You Don't Find Love, You Create Love" Sharon Esther Lampert

# My Self-Love Notes
## The Most Important Relationship Is the One You Have with Yourself
## Self-Love Is a Daily Practice

"You Don't Find Love, You Create Love" Sharon Esther Lampert

# My Self-Love Notes
### The Most Important Relationship Is the One You Have with Yourself
### Self-Love Is a Daily Practice

"You Don't Find Love, You Create Love" Sharon Esther Lampert

# My Self-Love Notes
## The Most Important Relationship Is the One You Have with Yourself
## Self-Love Is a Daily Practice

"You Don't Find Love, You Create Love" Sharon Esther Lampert

# My Self-Love Notes
## The Most Important Relationship Is the One You Have with Yourself
## Self-Love Is a Daily Practice

"You Don't Find Love, You Create Love" Sharon Esther Lampert

# My Self-Love Notes
## The Most Important Relationship Is the One You Have with Yourself
## Self-Love Is a Daily Practice

"You Don't Find Love, You Create Love" Sharon Esther Lampert

# My Self-Love Notes
## The Most Important Relationship Is the One You Have with Yourself
## Self-Love Is a Daily Practice

"You Don't Find Love, You Create Love" Sharon Esther Lampert

# My Self-Love Notes
### The Most Important Relationship Is the One You Have with Yourself
### Self-Love Is a Daily Practice

"You Don't Find Love, You Create Love" Sharon Esther Lampert

# My Self-Love Notes
## The Most Important Relationship Is the One You Have with Yourself
## Self-Love Is a Daily Practice

"You Don't Find Love, You Create Love" Sharon Esther Lampert

# My Self-Love Notes
## The Most Important Relationship Is the One You Have with Yourself
## Self-Love Is a Daily Practice

"You Don't Find Love, You Create Love" Sharon Esther Lampert

# My Self-Love Notes
### The Most Important Relationship Is the One You Have with Yourself
### Self-Love Is a Daily Practice

"You Don't Find Love, You Create Love" Sharon Esther Lampert

# My Self-Love Notes
### The Most Important Relationship Is the One You Have with Yourself
### Self-Love Is a Daily Practice

"You Don't Find Love, You Create Love." Sharon Esther Lampert

# My Self-Love Notes
## The Most Important Relationship Is the One You Have with Yourself
## Self-Love Is a Daily Practice

"You Don't Find Love, You Create Love" Sharon Esther Lampert

# My Self-Love Notes
## The Most Important Relationship Is the One You Have with Yourself
## Self-Love Is a Daily Practice

"You Don't Find Love, You Create Love" Sharon Esther Lampert

# My Self-Love Notes
## The Most Important Relationship Is the One You Have with Yourself
## Self-Love Is a Daily Practice

"You Don't Find Love, You Create Love" Sharon Esther Lampert

# My Self-Love Notes
## The Most Important Relationship Is the One You Have with Yourself
## Self-Love Is a Daily Practice

"You Don't Find Love, You Create Love" Sharon Esther Lampert

# My Self-Love Notes
## The Most Important Relationship Is the One You Have with Yourself
## Self-Love Is a Daily Practice

"You Don't Find Love, You Create Love" Sharon Esther Lampert

# My Self-Love Notes
## The Most Important Relationship Is the One You Have with Yourself
## Self-Love Is a Daily Practice

"You Don't Find Love, You Create Love" Sharon Esther Lampert

# My Self-Love Notes
## The Most Important Relationship Is the One You Have with Yourself
## Self-Love Is a Daily Practice

"You Don't Find Love, You Create Love" Sharon Esther Lampert

# My Self-Love Notes
## The Most Important Relationship Is the One You Have with Yourself
## Self-Love Is a Daily Practice

"You Don't Find Love, You Create Love" Sharon Esther Lampert

# My Self-Love Notes
## The Most Important Relationship Is the One You Have with Yourself
## Self-Love Is a Daily Practice

"You Don't Find Love, You Create Love" Sharon Esther Lampert

# My Self-Love Notes
### The Most Important Relationship Is the One You Have with Yourself
### Self-Love Is a Daily Practice

"You Don't Find Love, You Create Love" Sharon Esther Lampert

# My Self-Love Notes
## The Most Important Relationship Is the One You Have with Yourself
## Self-Love Is a Daily Practice

"You Don't Find Love, You Create Love" Sharon Esther Lampert

# My Self-Love Notes
## The Most Important Relationship Is the One You Have with Yourself
## Self-Love Is a Daily Practice

"You Don't Find Love, You Create Love" Sharon Esther Lampert

# My Self-Love Notes
## The Most Important Relationship Is the One You Have with Yourself
## Self-Love Is a Daily Practice

"You Don't Find Love, You Create Love" Sharon Esther Lampert

# My Self-Love Notes
## The Most Important Relationship Is the One You Have with Yourself
## Self-Love Is a Daily Practice

"You Don't Find Love, You Create Love" Sharon Esther Lampert

www.ingramcontent.com/pod-product-compliance
Lightning Source LLC
LaVergne TN
LVHW070121080526
838201LV00095B/251